BIBLICAL SONGS ILLUMINATED

G.E. MULLAN
JOHN SHEA

WORLD LIBRARY PUBLICATIONS

Franklin Park, Illinois

Canticle: Biblical Songs Illuminated © 2009, World Library Publications, the music and liturgy division of J. S. Paluch Company, Inc., 3708 River Road, Suite 400, Franklin Park, Illinois 60131-2158
800 566-6150 www.wlpmusic.com

All rights reserved under United States copyright law. No part of this book may be reproduced or transmitted in any form or by any means, whether mechanical, photographic, or electronic, including photocopying, or any information storage or retrieval system, without the written permission of the appropriate copyright owner.

Excerpts from the *New American Bible with Revised New Testament and Psalms,* Copyright © 1991, 1986, 1970, Confraternity of Christian Doctrine, Inc , Washington, DC. Used with permission. All rights reserved. No portion of the *New American Bible* may be reprinted without permission in writing from the copyright holder.

Art by G. E. Mullan; meditations by John Shea.

This book was edited by Michael E. Novak. Marcia T. Lucey was the copy editor.
Graphic design and layout by Christine Enault. Production manager was Deb Johnston.
Director of Publications: Mary Beth Kunde-Anderson. The book was set in ITC New Baskerville and Kepler. Printed in the United States of America.

WLP 017347

ISBN 978-1-58459-427-7

For Celina,
"love is the whole and more than all"
—G. E. M.

Gratitude from a non-singer
to all the singers
who have lifted my soul.
—J. S.

Preface

While the narratives in the Bible retell the events of God's actions in the history of the Chosen People, it is the songs, canticles, and laments in scripture that best express the personal and human reaction of God's people to those events.

Scripture scholars hold that most of these canticles were actually recorded before the narratives to which they are related were written, leaving us to realize that it was the human response to the event that propelled the cultural need to capture that event in story. The canticles are earlier vessels of these events, more primitive versions of them, and as such are closer to the cultic life of God's people.

Contemporary visual presentation of the canticles through artistic form is a critical part of our Christian tradition; art interprets faith and enables the faithful to keep alive and dynamic the faith that sustains life.

—G. E. Mullan

Exodus 15:1–21

Moses and the Israelites sang this song to the LORD:

I will sing to the LORD, for he is gloriously triumphant;
    horse and chariot he has cast into the sea.
My strength and my courage is the LORD,
    and he has been my savior.
He is my God, I praise him;
    the God of my father, I extol him.
The LORD is a warrior,
    LORD is his name!
Pharaoh's chariots and army he hurled into the sea;
    the elite of his officers were submerged in the Red Sea.

The flood waters covered them,
    they sank into the depths like a stone.
Your right hand, O LORD, magnificent in power,
    your right hand, O LORD, has shattered the enemy.
In your great majesty you overthrew your adversaries;
    you loosed your wrath to consume them like stubble.
At a breath of your anger the waters piled up,
    the flowing waters stood like a mound,
    the flood waters congealed in the midst of the sea.

The enemy boasted, "I will pursue and overtake them;
    I will divide the spoils and have my fill of them;
    I will draw my sword; my hand shall despoil them!"
When your wind blew, the sea covered them;
    like lead they sank in the mighty waters.

Who is like to you among the gods, O LORD?
    Who is like to you, magnificent in holiness?
O terrible in renown, worker of wonders,
    when you stretched out your right hand,
    the earth swallowed them!

In your mercy you led the people you redeemed;
    in your strength you guided them
    to your holy dwelling.
The nations heard and quaked;
    anguish gripped the dwellers in Philistia.
Then were the princes of Edom dismayed;
    trembling seized the chieftains of Moab;
All the dwellers in Canaan melted away;
    terror and dread fell upon them.
By the might of your arm they were frozen like stone,
    while your people, O LORD, passed over,
    while the people you had made your own passed over.

And you brought them in and planted them
    on the mountain of your inheritance—
    the place where you made your seat, O LORD,
    the sanctuary, O LORD,
    which your hands established.

The LORD shall reign forever and ever.

They sang thus because Pharaoh's horses and chariots and charioteers had gone into the sea, and the LORD made the waters of the sea flow back upon them, though the Israelites had marched on dry land through the midst of the sea. The prophetess Miriam, Aaron's sister, took a tambourine in her hand, while all the women went out after her with tambourines, dancing; and she led them in the refrain:

Sing to the LORD, for he is gloriously triumphant;
    horse and chariot he has cast into the sea.

When I sing this canticle of freed slaves,
I pay a visit to Miriam.
She hangs in the entrance to our apartment,
a 16 x 13-inch sculpting on a 22 x 18-inch board.
She wears a blue skirt, gray shirt, and gold belt.
A stole, decorated with Jewish symbols,
hangs around her neck.
She does not have two tambourines
as does the lovely Miriam you see here.
But she radiates the same gracious strength.
Everything about her says
"Victory."

    I bought the piece from a local artist
      and gave it to the woman
        I would eventually marry.
          The attached note read:
            "The Daughter of God plays in the storm."
       Although we have redecorated the entrance
         many times,
            my wife insists that
              Miriam stay at the threshold,
                greeting whoever comes among us.

Miriam, in turn, reminds me
of a rounded copper shield
with a butterfly embossed on it.
It was a gift from a woman
who received it from no less a personage
    than Fidel Castro
for her work with the poor women of Cuba.
She gave me the shield with the pointed observation,
"Butterflies break out of whatever confines them."

That is the undying truth of the canticle.
We are not meant to be enslaved.
We are daughters and sons of God,
and even though storms engulf us,
we will dance on the far side of the Red Sea.
No matter the strength of what restricts us,
our butterfly natures will fly us to freedom.
No pharaohs of Egypt,
no princes of Edom,
no chieftains of Moab,
no dwellers in Philistia and Canaan
can ever completely crush this sense of destiny.
It resides in the marrow bone.

*Yet slavery's sure defeat
does not stop us from trafficking in oppression.
The desire to possess people,
the dark drive to own people
stubbornly survives.
It is a twisted strand
in the double helix of the soul.
It has the power to enthrall us
without our knowing it.
It is never explicit, always beneath the surface,
the atmosphere, coloration, and tone
of every interaction.
Even our smiles are affected.*

*When our egos swell,
we want to be obeyed,
quickly, completely, and without question.
When we make others subservient,
we thrill to the inner rush of power.
When they do our will and not their own,
we puff with importance.
We are somebody to be reckoned with.
The prophets may shout,
"In enslaving others, you enslave yourself,"
but we ignore them.
Whatever the achievements of "civilization" may be,
we have not shaken
the ancient addiction to domination.*

*But the canticle is clear:
The outer forms and
    inner drives of slavery
will not last.
God is unalterably
    opposed to slavery
and Divine Patience
    will wear down human sin.
Make no mistake about it,
the horse and chariot
    will be cast into the sea.
But until that day of liberation,
while freedom is still ours
and choice confronts us,
let us sing this canticle
in the spirit of the word
    that God spoke
through Moses
to all slave-holders:
"Let my people go!"*

2 Samuel 6:11-23

The ark of the Lord remained in the house of Obed-edom the Gittite for three months, and the Lord blessed Obed-edom and his whole house. When it was reported to King David that the Lord had blessed the family of Obed-edom and all that belonged to him, David went to bring up the ark of God from the house of Obed-edom into the City of David amid festivities. As soon as the bearers of the ark of the Lord had advanced six steps, he sacrificed an ox and a fatling. Then David, girt with a linen apron, came dancing before the Lord with abandon, as he and all the Israelites were bringing up the ark of the Lord with shouts of joy and to the sound of the horn. As the ark of the Lord was entering the City of David, Saul's daughter Michal looked down through the window and saw King David leaping and dancing before the Lord, and she despised him in her heart. The ark of the Lord was brought in and set in its place within the tent David had pitched for it. Then David offered holocausts and peace offerings before the Lord. When he finished making these offerings, he blessed the people in the name of the Lord of hosts. He then distributed among all the people, to each man and each woman in the entire multitude of Israel, a loaf of bread, a cut of roast meat, and a raisin cake. With this, all the people left for their homes.

When David returned to bless his own family, Saul's daughter Michal came out to meet him and said, "How the king of Israel has honored himself today, exposing himself to the view of the slave girls of his followers, as a commoner might do!" But David replied to Michal: "I was dancing before the Lord. As the Lord lives, who preferred me to your father and his whole family when he appointed me commander of the Lord's people, Israel, not only will I make merry before the Lord, but I will demean myself even more. I will be lowly in your esteem, but in the esteem of the slave girls you spoke of I will be honored." And so Saul's daughter Michal was childless to the day of her death.

When I read
of David "dancing before the Lord with abandon,"
I see him in my mind's eye
as he appears here,
leaping and whirling,
leading others in the procession
that brings the Ark to Jerusalem.

David dancing, in turn, reminds me
of a painting that hangs in our family room.
It is entitled "Spirited Dance."
A large woman,
perhaps African, perhaps not,
wrapped in green, gold, and black,
is radiantly shaking.
Her eyes are wide open,
mesmerized by the sight
   of something
      only she can see.
         Her face is transported with joy.
            Everything she is
               is moving through her body.

Are not David and this woman
what we want?
We desire Spirit to be released
from the secret center of our soul
to elevate our mind,
inhabit our body,
and turn every toenail to ballet.
We want embodied ecstasy,
nothing held back,
everything manifested.
We dwell indoors too much,
hunched in a cramped space,
basically unborn from the womb.

We need to stretch, spread, leap,
Baryshnikov for a moment.
Our tightly tied hair
yearns to be let down,
shoulder length,
combed by our beloved's fingers.

What good is our faith
if it does not bring us to dance?
What good are our bold beliefs
if they do not make irresistible music?
What good is our virtue
if it does not move in rhythm with the wind?
When the Ark comes home,
it is housed in our heart
and only the heart,
with all its passion unleashed,
can display it.
If Dante is right,
God does not dwell
in frozen places.

The David in us,
however,
moving in the embrace of grace,
is despised by Michal,
who watches without sleep
from the upper window of our mind.
She resents the play of our feet upon the earth.
She detests our rapture.
We cannot argue her down
or entice her to join the dance.
The queen cannot give herself
to the pleasure that slave girls love.
We will have to leap in full view of her looking,
not allowing her disdain to dampen our fire.
We are told Michal bore no children.
Life never moved in her.

But life moves in us,
bread, roasted meat, and raisin cakes
in the circle of our friends and families,
the sound of horns in our ears,
shouts of joy in the air,
the tambourine on our hip—
sinuously attuned to the Spirit's music—
God's homecoming and our own.

Tobit 13:1-8

Then Tobit composed this joyful prayer:

Blessed be God who lives forever,
    because his kingdom lasts for all ages.
For he scourges and then has mercy;
    he casts down to the depths of the nether world,
    and he brings up from the great abyss.
No one can escape his hand.

Praise him, you Israelites, before the Gentiles,
    for though he has scattered you among them,
    he has shown you his greatness even there.
Exalt him before every living being,
    because he is the Lord our God,
    our Father and God forever.
He scourged you for your iniquities,
    but will again have mercy on you all.
He will gather you from all the Gentiles
    among whom you have been scattered.

When you turn back to him with all your heart,
    to do what is right before him,
Then he will turn back to you,
    and no longer hide his face from you.

So now consider what he has done for you,
    and praise him with full voice.
Bless the Lord of righteousness,
    and exalt the King of the ages.

In the land of my exile I praise him,
    and show his power and majesty to a sinful nation.
"Turn back, you sinners! do the right before him:
    perhaps he may look with favor upon you
    and show you mercy.

"As for me, I exalt my God,
    and my spirit rejoices in the King of heaven.
Let all men speak of his majesty,
    and sing his praises in Jerusalem."

When I sing this canticle of elder Tobit,
I remember, half-smiling, the series of events
that brought him to this overflowing praise.
He is a righteous man
who has been blinded by the droppings of a bird
and reduced to poverty.
He sends his son on a journey
to collect a longstanding debt.
(By the way, the dog went with him.)
The son is accompanied by a man
who turns out to be the angel Raphael.
Raphael instructs the younger Tobit
that the innards of a fish can cure blindness
and that prayer rather than lust
will win him the fair yet haunted Sarah.
The younger Tobit gets the money and the girl,
and the elder Tobit sees again.
It is time to bless the Lord of righteousness.

But I wonder about the scenarios of Tobit's song.
How do the lost get found?
How do those who have strayed return?
How do the scourged receive mercy?
Just what does it mean
for sinners to turn back to the Lord?
How do they come face to face
when for so long they have been back to back?

Who makes the first move—
God or the sinner,
the Creator or the estranged creature,
the Parent or the lost son or daughter?

When the prodigal son is in the pigsty,
he comes to his senses
and turns toward the house of his father.
While still a long way off,
his father sees him and begins to run.
The lost son makes the first move,
but it is only the slightest of moves,
a first step.
Yet it is matched by a gallop,
by the all-out run of the father.
This is how it is:
we barely turn and God is on us,
kissing us, weeping down our necks,
ordering servants to bring us
robes, rings, and sandals,
announcing the fate of the fatted calf.
We do not have to crawl the whole way back.
All we have to do is turn.
God's mercy needs only the slightest opening.

But it is trickier than that.
We do not know our true condition
until we are moving out of it.
Before the first step
our consciousness is so false that
we think lost is found, death is life,
darkness is light, asleep is awake.
We are far from God,
but we do not know it.

Then something happens.
A friend dies,
a child smiles us into wonder,
an adolescent yells at us,
we suddenly remember the food
    in our father's house,
a secret weakness is painfully revealed,
we are unexpectedly kissed,
our comforting self-image is shaken,
the market falls,
we blithely achieve what we least wanted.
There is no end to things that happen.

If we look closely,
we will see that every turning back to God
is a response to things that happen,
either internal or external.
And if we look more closely
at that first step, however short or long,
we will discern an urging at its center,
a call that was so unassuming
we did not bother to refuse it.
Only in retrospect will we see
the call was also a judgment
    on where we were,
its light showing us our darkness,
its life showing us our death.
By the time we know we are lost,
we have already been found.

As Tobit intuits,
this consciousness
    causes us to rejoice,
for reasons we may not be able
    to name completely.
But we smile with recognition
when we are told that
God whispered to the mystic:
"You would not be seeking Me
if I had not first found you."

Judith 16:1–17

"Strike up the instruments,
    a song to my God with timbrels,
        chant to the LORD with cymbals;
Sing to him a new song,
    exalt and acclaim his name.
For the LORD is God; he crushes warfare,
    and sets his encampment among his people;
        he snatched me from the hands of my persecutors.

"The Assyrian came from the mountains of the north,
    with the myriads of his forces he came;
Their numbers blocked the torrents, their horses
        covered the hills.
He threatened to burn my land,
    put my youths to the sword,
Dash my babes to the ground,
    make my children a prey,
    and seize my virgins as spoil.

"But the LORD Almighty thwarted them,
    by a woman's hand he confounded them.
Not by youths was their mighty one struck down,
    nor did titans bring him low,
    nor huge giants attack him;
But Judith, the daughter of Merari,
    by the beauty of her countenance disabled him.
She took off her widow's garb
    to raise up the afflicted in Israel.
She anointed her face with fragrant oil;
    with a fillet she fastened her tresses,
    and put on a linen robe to beguile him.
Her sandals caught his eyes,
    and her beauty captivated his mind.
    The sword cut through his neck.

"The Persians were dismayed at her daring,
    the Medes appalled at her boldness.
When my lowly ones shouted, they were terrified;
    when my weaklings cried out, they trembled;
    at the sound of their war cry, they took to flight.
The sons of slave girls pierced them through;
    the supposed sons of rebel mothers cut them down;
    they perished before the ranks of my LORD.

"A new hymn I will sing to my God.
    O LORD, great are you and glorious,
    wonderful in power and unsurpassable.
Let your every creature serve you;
    for you spoke, and they were made,
You sent forth your spirit, and they were created;
    no one can resist your word.
The mountains to their bases, and the seas, are shaken;
    the rocks, like wax, melt before your glance.

"But to those who fear you,
    you are very merciful.
Though the sweet odor of every sacrifice is a trifle,
    and the fat of all holocausts but little in your sight,
    one who fears the Lord is forever great.

"Woe to the nations that rise against my people!
    The LORD Almighty will requite them;
    in the day of judgment he will punish them:
He will send fire and worms into their flesh,
    and they shall burn and suffer forever."

When I sing this canticle of and about Judith,
I cannot get past the fact that
it took her two whacks
with Holofernes' own sword
to sever his head from his body.
Her weak widow arms
could not accomplish the salvation of her people
with one full, clean swing.
The two blows have theological import.

Judith, the proximate player, struck the first blow:
God, the ultimate actor, provided the strength
of the decisive blow.
Therefore,
when the victory is celebrated in song,
the lyrics must be:
"The Lord Almighty . . .
by a woman's hand . . .
confounded [the Assyrians]."
 Two interlocked actors are acknowledged,
 one the source and one the means.

Judith is a widow—
a sexy, savvy, gutsy, wily widow—
but a widow nonetheless.
She belongs to one of the groups
whom God both protects and uses
to accomplish divine purposes.
During prayer, Judith has the chutzpah
to remind God of this preference.
"Your strength is not in numbers,
nor does your power depend upon stalwart men;
but you are the God of the lowly,
 the helper of the oppressed,
the supporter of the weak,
 the protector of the forsaken,
the savior of those without hope" (9:11).

This theology spills over into an argument.
If Jeremiah stutters
and still produces jeremiads . . .
if Gideon is a mediocre warrior
and still wins battles . . .
if Elizabeth is barren
and still gives birth . . .
if Judith is a widow
and still overcomes the general
of the massive war machine of Assyria . . .
then the only explanation is:
God is working through their weakness
to confound the strength of the socially dominant.

But more is at work in this song of liberation
than God's way of working through weakness.
Much is made of how Judith's beauty
captivated the mind of Holofernes.
But it was more her speech than her appearance
that made the mental processes of Holofernes
work against him.
Judith so successfully played into his narcissism
that he tells his servant,
"It would be a disgrace for us to have
   such a woman with us
without enjoying her company.
If we do not entice her, she will laugh us to scorn" (12:12).
Lust is always a factor,
but the real driver of Holofernes' drunkenness
   and death
is his egotism—his fear of disgrace and laughter.

Oppressors have the seeds of destruction
already planted in them.
Widows, representing all the vulnerable,
know how to water them.
God working from the underside of history
and the upperside of history
   working against itself
is a potent mix.
It leads to considerable pondering,
and for those with a penchant for
   end-time thinking,
it recalls the least
   understood
but perhaps best-bet
   prophecy of the
   scriptures:
The meek shall inherit
   the earth.

Psalm 42:2-12

As the deer longs for streams of water,
    so my soul longs for you, O God.
My being thirsts for God, the living God.
    When can I go and see the face of God?
My tears have been my food day and night,
    as they ask daily, "Where is your God?"
Those times I recall
    as I pour out my soul,
When I went in procession with the crowd,
    I went with them to the house of God,
Amid loud cries of thanksgiving,
    with the multitude keeping festival.
Why are you downcast, my soul;
    why do you groan within me?
Wait for God, whom I shall praise again,
    my savior and my God.

My soul is downcast within me;
    therefore I will remember you
From the land of the Jordan and Hermon,
    from the land of Mount Mizar.
Here deep calls to deep in the roar of your torrents.
    All your waves and breakers sweep over me.
At dawn may the Lord bestow faithful love
    that I may sing praise through the night,
    praise to the God of my life.
I say to God, "My rock,
    why do you forget me?
Why must I go about mourning
    with the enemy oppressing me?"
It shatters my bones, when my adversaries
      reproach me.
    They say to me daily: "Where is your God?"
Why are you downcast, my soul,
    why do you groan within me?
Wait for God, whom I shall praise again,
    my savior and my God.

When I sing this canticle,
I know it is everyone's song.
Who,
in the course of their lives
or in their worst imaginings
or in both,
has not been there?

Who has not been so consumed by pain and loss
that their tears took the place of food?
Who has not previously praised,
"in procession with the crowd"
the God who now is nowhere to be found?
Who has not felt the rock
upon which they stood
swept away with the "roar of [the] torrents"?

If you do not admit this,
we will brand you saint or liar,
and there is room for neither
in the frail and frightened band
who sing this song.
We are wafflers,
believer and unbeliever in one skin.
We do not need enemies to taunt us,
mocking our misplaced faith.
We do that for ourselves.

That is why the canticle's solution is not for me.
I cannot hunker down and wait for rescue.
I cannot pit a stubborn faith
against prolonged absence.
I am afraid prolonged absence will win.
The coward in me is always sniffing out
a more delicate perfume,
a more subtle presence.

The Sufi master Rumi concocts a fragrance
from the very absence of what we long for:
We are like "love dogs" moaning for our master,
    he says.
Our whining connects us to God.
Any prayer of absence assumes
the presence of the One who is not there.

There is something to that.
But it is not the longed-for presence,
the presence that will change our situation.
It is not intervention.

*Intervention died on the cross of Christ.
The crowds mistook his cry to God
as a call to Elijah to come and take him down.
In their eagerness for spectacle,
they sponged sour wine into his mouth
    to keep him alive
so the delayed Elijah could arrive
    from heaven on his chariot.
Jesus did not accommodate their miracle-mongering.
With a loud cry he breathed his last.*

*I take Jesus' embrace of death—
his loud cry and breathing forth his breath—
to be another way,
an alternative to rescue
yet something more than mere presence.*

*As we sink beneath the waves,
might we find restful waters that support us?
As the outer world tears at us,
might an inner world hold our frightened hearts
with such steadiness that a loud cry
can come forth from shattered bones?
Might surrender be a form of transcendence?*

*I ask such questions about this hope
because my un-evolved animal mind
will never have first-hand awareness
of so awesome and graceful a possibility.
But if the Darkness is ultimately Love
(and I cannot bring myself to believe it is not),
I know the Mystery would want to be
with downcast souls,
even if those souls
    could not feel a presence
so subtle
that it would not break
    the bruised reed
or quench the smoldering wick.*

*We are deer,
parched for living water,
but all too often
we are given only sour wine.
Might it be true
that an inner fountain,
the Being of our being,
springs up to slake our thirst,
if we but knew how to turn
and drink?*

Psalm 47:2-10

All you peoples, clap your hands,
    shout to God with cries of gladness,
For the Lord, the Most High, the awesome,
    is the great king over all the earth.
He brings peoples under us;
    nations under our feet.
He chooses for us our inheritance,
    the glory of Jacob, whom he loves.

God mounts his throne amid shouts of joy;
    the Lord, amid trumpet blasts.
Sing praise to God, sing praise;
    sing praise to our King, sing praise.

For King of all the earth is God;
    sing hymns of praise.
God reigns over the nations,
    God sits upon his holy throne.
The princes of the peoples are gathered together
    with the people of the God of Abraham.
For God's are the guardians of the earth;
    he is supreme.

When I sing this canticle,
I remember all the times I have clapped my hands,
when I have put two palms together
to praise what was excellent
and let the world know,
a world that had previously been in doubt,
that a spirit lives in my flesh.

However,
my life of clapping has not been pure.
I have applauded when I did not mean it.
Perfunctory. Expected. Polite.
And I have clapped
when I was not sure why.
As my hands were coming together
and pulling apart,
was I praising someone's victory
or taking delight in someone's defeat?
And I have been sullen,
refusing admiration,
walking past quiet marvels
with my hands resolutely sunk
in pockets.
My history of applause is checkered.
How about yours?

The canticle thinks
contemplating God as king of the earth
will get us to shout, "Awesome!"
But what if we throw our mind into time and space
and entertain the whole universe?
Clapping is bound to follow.
And it is about time.

I think the universe.
may suffer from under-appreciation,
reduced to mere backdrop,
only scenery for the human adventure.
Nature, for all its inexorable laws
and its reputation for endurance,
may really be a continuous divine play,
performed daily in response
to the one prayer humans always ask
and the one prayer God cannot refuse:
"Encore! Encore!"
Perhaps it is only
when we put our hands together
for God's handiwork
that the sun also rises—
or, to be scientifically correct—
the earth turns.
Ovation may prevent collapse.

*I like applause
when it is accompanied by mouth sounds.
I value those people,
although I am not one of them,
who when they clap,
let off for a moment
and put one hand into their mouth
and produce a shrill whistle.
This cacophony is needed
to prove chaos
is as much a part of God
as order.
When we are carried away,
we readily sacrifice decorum to excitement.
Runaway bliss does not consult Miss Manners.*

*But total body praise is not easy for me.
I grew up in dark and silent Gothic churches
that knew their way around my mind
and regularly raised it
into their symbolic ceilings.
The mind in God is
Ecstasy!*

*But once I rocked with the Daughters of Isabella
to Gospel music that knew its way around my body.
The mouth, hands, and feet in God is
Exuberance!*

*Someone said,
"People don't want to know
the meaning of life.
They want an experience of being alive."
Intense aliveness stops
the questioning of the mind.
The gladdened heart seeks expression,
not answers.
I would rather be clacking hand cymbals
than questing for certitude.*

*Nothing is better
than when foot stomping,
hand clapping,
mouth moving
cannot but start.
In those times
we become instruments of Spirit,
divine music gushing out
in joyful human ways.
Even the unmusical
put a trumpet to their lips
and blast.*

Psalm 137:1-4

By the rivers of Babylon
    we sat mourning and weeping
    when we remembered Zion.
On the poplars of that land
    we hung up our harps.
There our captors asked us
    for the words of a song;
Our tormentors, for a joyful song:
    "Sing for us a song of Zion!"
But how could we sing a song of the Lord
    in a foreign land?

When I sing this canticle of tears—
an expression of sadness so deep
that the only request for joy
comes from tormentors,
an expression of sadness so deep
it cannot pretend songs from Zion
could ever turn Babylon into home—
I sense the secret purpose of grief.

Zion is not one more city.
It is the spiritual home of these mourners,
the place where God dwells with people
    and people live in peace with each other.
      When we are not in that home,
        when we are alienated from God
        and one another,
          we cannot sing,
          for songs of the Lord
            must come
        from communion with
          the Lord.
      Nothing can make up for
        the absence.

But we are always tempted to try.
To live in separation is painful,
and we are quick to medicate hurt.
As soon as possible,
we find remedies for negative inner states.
Time will heal,
we say.
We must make the best
of a bad situation,
we say.
Resignation is our only refuge,
we say.

We transform our theology
into bandages and balm.
God is not tied to one place,
we say.
Perhaps we have lost the fullness of God and people,
but God is present even in a foreign land,
we say.
If we sing, the faint divine presence
will become louder,
we say.
Advocates advise that
this practical approach will dry our tears.

*But what if there were another way,
a path beyond adaptation to loss?
What if the refusal to sing
is the way Zion is remembered?
What if the harps hanging from trees
preserve our love for the reality of home
and do not let us settle for a substitute?
What if there is a strength of character
that can integrate incompleteness
without letting emptiness lead to despair?*

*There is a story about a rebbe
talking to his disciples
but not finding them receptive.
He explained the existence of God.
    Not one of them understood.
He illumined God's presence in creation.
    Not one of them understood.
He spoke of insatiable longing for God.
    All nodded.*

*   The secret purpose of grief:
                      Longing keeps love alive.*

Song of Songs 2:8–13

Hark! my lover—here he comes
    springing across the mountains,
    leaping across the hills.
My lover is like a gazelle
    or a young stag.
Here he stands behind our wall,
    gazing through the windows,
    peering through the lattices.
My lover speaks; he says to me,
    "Arise, my beloved, my beautiful one,
    and come!
"For see, the winter is past,
    the rains are over and gone.
The flowers appear on the earth,
    the time of pruning the vines has come,
    and the song of the dove is heard in our land.
The fig tree puts forth its figs,
    and the vines, in bloom, give forth fragrance.
Arise, my beloved, my beautiful one,
    and come!"

When I sing this canticle of love,
    my old body aches with memories of times past
when a comparison to a young stag
    would not bring laughter,
when romance could leap mountains,
    turn winter into spring,
    and rival figs and flowers for fragrance.

But now love does not pant outside walls
    or peek through lattices.
    It is a series of small showings,
      a dropping of veils to reveal beauty.

For she is never more beautiful than
    in my office,
    clearing the briefcase from the chair,
    sitting in winter leather and jeans,
    smiling
into the chaos of books,
each of her words
a lifeline to my sinking soul.

For she is never more beautiful than
when I am leaning against the wall
at C27
in an airport far away from where I want to be.
I ring up with abrupt telegraph intentions.
"Will be late." Stop.
She upturns a bottle of syrup,
a slow, thick pour of her day,
hour-by-hour sweetness.
And then she gets it.
"This is not the time." Stop
"Whenever you get here." Stop.
"Bye." Stop.
"Kiss." Stop.
The phone is dead. Stop.
And I am left loved. Stop.
In the only way I could be. Stop.

*For she is never more beautiful than
insisting, "Let's do your nose."
I lie on the bed,
my head hanging off,
my nostrils skyward
as the tear-shaped steroids
drop from the bottle,
splashing balm on swelling sinuses.
And then
the Shekinah of her lips descends,
brushing the mountaintop of my nose,
and the voice of the turtledove
is heard in the land, whispering,
"Now for the real medicine."*

*Hark!
Is that the turn of the key in the door
that I hear?
She is home.
Bounding through the kitchen,
leaping over the dining room table,
my lover comes to me.
She speaks:*
    *"Arise, my beloved,
    my beautiful one,
    and come!"*
*Using both arms,
my knees creaking,
with a mighty effort
pushing out of my chair,
I arise and come.*

Daniel 3:52-90

"Blessed are you, O Lord, the God of our fathers,
    praiseworthy and exalted above all forever;
And blessed is your holy and glorious name,
    praiseworthy and exalted above all for all ages.
Blessed are you in the temple of your holy glory,
    praiseworthy and glorious above all forever.
Blessed are you on the throne of your kingdom,
    praiseworthy and exalted above all forever.
Blessed are you who look into the depths
    from your throne upon the cherubim,
    praiseworthy and exalted above all forever.
Blessed are you in the firmament of heaven,
    praiseworthy and glorious forever.
Bless the Lord, all you works of the Lord,
    praise and exalt him above all forever.
Angels of the Lord, bless the Lord,
    praise and exalt him above all forever.
You heavens, bless the Lord,
    praise and exalt him above all forever.
All you waters above the heavens, bless the Lord,
    praise and exalt him above all forever.
All you hosts of the Lord, bless the Lord;
    praise and exalt him above all forever.
Sun and moon, bless the Lord;
    praise and exalt him above all forever.
Stars of heaven, bless the Lord;
    praise and exalt him above all forever.
Every shower and dew, bless the Lord;
    praise and exalt him above all forever.
All you winds, bless the Lord;
    praise and exalt him above all forever.
Fire and heat, bless the Lord;
    praise and exalt him above all forever.
[Cold and chill, bless the Lord;
    praise and exalt him above all forever.
Dew and rain, bless the Lord;
    praise and exalt him above all forever.]
Frost and chill, bless the Lord;
    praise and exalt him above all forever.
Ice and snow, bless the Lord;
    praise and exalt him above all forever.
Nights and days, bless the Lord;
    praise and exalt him above all forever.
Light and darkness, bless the Lord;
    praise and exalt him above all forever.
Lightnings and clouds, bless the Lord;
    praise and exalt him above all forever.
Let the earth bless the Lord,
    praise and exalt him above all forever.
Mountains and hills, bless the Lord;
    praise and exalt him above all forever.
Everything growing from the earth, bless the Lord;
    praise and exalt him above all forever.
You springs, bless the Lord;
    praise and exalt him above all forever.
Seas and rivers, bless the Lord;
    praise and exalt him above all forever.
You dolphins and all water creatures, bless the Lord;
    praise and exalt him above all forever.
All you birds of the air, bless the Lord;
    praise and exalt him above all forever.
All you beasts, wild and tame, bless the Lord;
    praise and exalt him above all forever.
You sons of men, bless the Lord;
    praise and exalt him above all forever.

O Israel, bless the Lord;
    praise and exalt him above all forever.
Priests of the Lord, bless the Lord;
    praise and exalt him above all forever.
Servants of the Lord, bless the Lord;
    praise and exalt him above all forever.
Spirits and souls of the just, bless the Lord;
    praise and exalt him above all forever.
Holy men of humble heart, bless the Lord;
    praise and exalt him above all forever.
Hananiah, Azariah, Mishael, bless the Lord;
    praise and exalt him above all forever.
For he has delivered us from the nether world,
    and saved us from the power of death;
He has freed us from the raging flame
    and delivered us from the fire.
Give thanks to the Lord, for he is good,
    for his mercy endures forever.
Bless the God of gods, all you who fear the Lord;
    praise him and give him thanks,
    because his mercy endures forever."

When I sing this canticle,
I try to get inside the courage and confidence
of Shadrach, Meshach, and Abednego,
who first "with one voice sang" (Daniel 3:51)
in less than ideal circumstances.
It is a stretch.

Nebuchadnezzar builds an image,
a golden colossus that all must worship.
He will not be the last
to erect an image for obeisance.
Caesar will demand a pinch of incense,
the Bishop will command an oath,
the CEO will insist on yes with a smile.
Idol-making is a perennial human activity.
Someone always wants
to make others bend
to what they have built.

The price of the failure to do homage
is to be thrown into the fiery furnace.
The furnace is heated seven times hotter than usual,
just in case added incentive is needed.

There is always a price
if we push back against the king.
It may be the loss of name, position, wealth, even life.
But there is always a fiery furnace
to test what we are made of,
always a peril to purify dross.

Of course,
most fall down and worship immediately.
Indeed, there is a rush to prostration.
That is why Nebuchadnezzar's face
becomes as hot as his furnace
when the three young men refuse to bow.

It is here that the mystery lies,
in this simple fact of resistance,
of valuing something more than life,
of pushing back against supreme social power.
It is this capacity—
our damnable conviction that we belong
to something more ultimate
than anything human hands can make—
that gets us into the trouble
we were born for.

That is essentially what the fiery furnace song,
with its litany of creatures, is all about.
The God of all creation is ultimate,
and every creature knows this
and blesses the Source
because their very being is tied to it.
To substitute something finite
for this infinite fountain
is to sever the link to life,
to lose your very self who is God's gift.
The three young men enter the furnace
wrapped in this incombustible truth.

Does this God of creation
deliver Shadrach,
Meshach, and Abednego
from the flames?
Does God send an angel
to make the high heat of the furnace
like a moist, whistling wind?
Do the young men walk out unharmed
at the king's bidding?
Does Nebuchadnezzar approve the God of the Jews?
Do Shadrach, Meshach, and Abednego
get promoted and their enemies get threatened
with being "cut to pieces" (3:96)?
The story says, "Yes!!!"
But we know that history,
over and over again,
has said, "No!"

By this time, however,
something has happened in the heart
that cannot be contradicted by adverse events.
Habakkuk knows what has happened.
> *"For though the fig tree blossom not*
>   *nor fruit be on the vines,*
> *Though the yield of the olive fail*
>   *and the terraces produce no nourishment,*
> *Though the flocks disappear from the fold,*
>   *and there be no herd in the stalls,*
> *yet I will rejoice in the L*ORD*" (Habakkuk 3:17–18).*

Daniel 6:26-28

Then King Darius wrote to the nations and peoples of every language, wherever they dwell on the earth: "All peace to you! I decree that throughout my royal domain the God of Daniel is to be reverenced and feared:

"For he is the living God, enduring forever;
    his kingdom shall not be destroyed,
    and his dominion shall be without end.
He is a deliverer and savior,
    working signs and wonders in heaven and on earth,
    and he delivered Daniel from the lions' power."

When I sing this canticle of King Darius,
I remember how happy he was
to issue this decree throughout the earth,
to sing to the God
whom Daniel showed him.

Daniel's enemies,
jealous of his blameless administration
    of Darius' domain,
plotted his downfall.
They had Darius issue an irrevocable decree:
only Darius could be prayed to.
The penalty for praying to anything else,
divine or human,
was to become lions' food.
But, of course, Daniel continued to face Jerusalem
and pray to the God of his people.
So his enemies reported him to Darius,
who was instantly distressed.
He did not want to doom Daniel,
but an irrevocable decree is an irrevocable decree.
          Daniel is thrown into the lions' den,
            accompanied by
              the king's ardent hope,
                "May your God,
                  whom you serve so constantly,
                  save you" (Daniel 6:17).

Darius is on Daniel's side.
He spends the night fasting
and at dawn hurries to the lions' den.
He cries out, "O Daniel, servant of the living God,
has the God whom you serve so constantly
been able to save you from the lions?" (6:21).
Daniel has a lot to say,
but basically the answer is, "Yes."
Darius is overjoyed,
and without prompting,
writes another irrevocable decree
that revokes the first irrevocable decree.
That is how it is
when you are dealing with the living God
whose kingdom knows no end
and who saves the innocent from evildoers.
Human decrees are transcended
    by divine interventions.

Darius wanted to believe in Daniel's God,
probably because of Daniel's stellar life.
But he needed a sign, and he got it:
an angel holding shut the mouths of lions.

We all look for signs,
whether we know it or not.
We want proof that a transcendent power
watches over the innocent,
and we fantasize that a miraculous deliverance
will bring us to the ecstatic faith of Darius' song.

However, while searching for signs,
I have been backed into a corner.
Better said, I have been backed into myself
because the outer world of signs and wonders,
even when they are spectacularly promoted,
leaves me without song.

But there is a love I feel,
a fierce commitment to those close to me
and by extension to all beings,
that I cannot attribute to my ego,
or to my conditioning, or to my fear,
or to any self-contained cause.

At times,
this love becomes a fountain within me,
a child kicking the womb for escape.
I play a silly game
of flowing with it and resisting it,
of letting it go and keeping it in.
But I cannot get myself to believe
it is not aligned with the Source of all things.
Saint Paul says love does not end;
but its powers are subtle.
It may be unable to close the mouths of lions,
but it fills me with song.

Jonah 2:1-11

But the LORD sent a large fish, that swallowed Jonah; and he remained in the belly of the fish three days and three nights. From the belly of the fish Jonah said this prayer to the LORD, his God:

Out of my distress I called to the LORD,
    and he answered me;
From the midst of the nether world I cried for help,
    and you heard my voice.
For you cast me into the deep, into the heart of the sea,
    and the flood enveloped me;
All your breakers and your billows
    passed over me.
Then I said, "I am banished from your sight!
    yet would I again look upon your holy temple."
The waters swirled about me, threatening my life;
    the abyss enveloped me;
    seaweed clung about my head.
Down I went to the roots of the mountains;
    the bars of the nether world
    were closing behind me forever,
But you brought up my life from the pit,
    O LORD, my God.

When my soul fainted within me,
    I remembered the LORD;
My prayer reached you
    in your holy temple.
Those who worship vain idols
    forsake their source of mercy.
But I, with resounding praise,
    will sacrifice to you;
What I have vowed I will pay:
    deliverance is from the LORD.

Then the LORD commanded the fish to spew Jonah upon the shore.

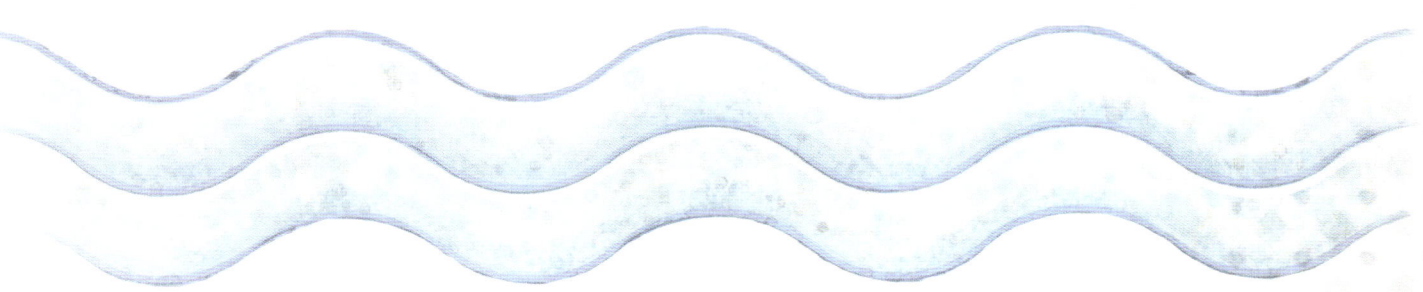

When I sing the canticle of Jonah,
I laugh at the whole hilarious tale.
I imagine him in his inspired moment
    of self-absorption,
composing this hymn in the belly of a whale,
a slippery place for a slippery man.

When the Lord asked Isaiah, "Whom shall I send?"
he said, without hesitating, "Send me!"
But when the Lord sent Jonah on a mission
    to Nineveh,
he booked a boat to Tarshish.
The Lord said, "Go east by land!"
Jonah went west by sea.

If our arms are too short to box with God,
our legs, even our sea legs, are too short
to run from God.

The Lord hurls a great wind
across the waters,
a tempestuous sea rises up
to block the escaping prophet.
The sailors are terrified
and they know whom to blame.

If the roiling sea wants Jonah,
so be it.
The sailors toss Jonah to the waves.
As he sinks toward the bottom,
the sea suddenly becomes calm.
The sailors are astonished:
their fear of the Lord worked.
Feed a reluctant prophet to the angry waters
and they cease to rage.
The sailors become believers,
offering sacrifices and making vows.
This is fun stuff.

Meanwhile,
Jonah is swallowed by a whale,
the Lord's sea taxi service.
In the safety of the whale's belly,
pondering his exploits
for three days and three nights,
Jonah carefully crafts a song of praise,
getting it half-right.

*Jonah extols the Lord for saving him
from the danger of drowning,
from a head wrapped round with seaweed,
from waters covering him,
from the bars of the nether world
clanking shut behind him.
This spectacular deliverance
has re-converted him to the source of mercy.
He promises he will worship only the Lord.
"[D]eliverance is from the L*ord*."*

*I am happy for his relief.
But this is standard stuff,
stock material for rescue prayers,
even the temple gets thrown in—liturgists rejoice.
However, it misses the point.*

*The Lord's response to the canticle
makes the point.
He commands the fish
to spew Jonah on the shore.
Once again, unceremoniously on dry land,
the Lord, for a* second *time, reminds Jonah
of what he is called to do.
The rescue is not important;
the mission is.*

*From beginning to end,
the God of prophets values performance
more than praise.
We never get this straight.
When we manage to dodge death,
we are ready to gush with gratitude,
sing a song of survival at the top our lungs,
and vow a better life.
Deliverance makes us giddy.*

*But the Lord not so patiently waits,
having marshaled winds, waters, and whales,
to get us to arrive once again
at the only place God is interested in,
the place from which we can
    no longer run
from the mission
    ordained for us
from the foundation
    of the world.
When we have finished
    our overblown aria,
the exasperated Word
    of the Lord arrives
    once again.
The first words are always
    the same:
"Now, about Nineveh!"*

Luke 1:46–55

And Mary said:

"My soul proclaims the greatness of the Lord;
>my spirit rejoices in God my savior.

For he has looked upon his handmaid's lowliness;
>behold, from now on will all ages call me blessed.

The Mighty One has done great things for me,
>and holy is his name.

His mercy is from age to age
>to those who fear him.

He has shown might with his arm,
>dispersed the arrogant of mind and heart.

He has thrown down the rulers from their thrones
>but lifted up the lowly.

The hungry he has filled with good things;
>the rich he has sent away empty.

He has helped Israel his servant,
>remembering his mercy,

according to his promise to our fathers,
>to Abraham and to his descendants forever."

When I sing this song of Mary,
I feel she takes my hand and leads me,
looking ahead at a path I cannot see.
Then she looks back,
checking my willingness,
making sure I am not pulling back—
or worse, turning back.

Although she does not say so,
her smile tells me
she is happy we are traveling together
and still more—
she cannot wait to show me
our destination.

Our journey is a descent inward and downward.
We pull away from the social traffic,
from the competitions of the outer world,
from the fray whose fights define me,
from the noise that smothers
the whisperings of the spirit.
I leave reluctantly.
This is the world I know.

Mary senses my foot-dragging.
She says, "We will return.
You will see it differently."

She closes her eyes
and I, her follower, do the same.
We enter the inner landscape of the body.
Every sensation is allowed,
every pleasure and pain embraced.
We float in the rivers of my veins.
Then another chamber opens.
We are on the balcony of the mind,
watching the dance of thought and feeling.
Everything is moving.
I could linger in these unfolding dramas.

But she is a step ahead,
urging me forward.
"We are almost there," she says.
"Where?" I ask.
She does not look at me.
Her pace has quickened.
"The place where the Spirit rejoices," she says.

Suddenly we are in the center
 without a circumference.
The umbilical cord to God is uncut;
divine life flows into us,
turning our lowliness into largeness,
magnifying the life that blesses us.
And everything that is
drives toward everything else that is.
We rest in holy communion.

"So this is the other side of fear," I say.
"Mercy," she says,
and the word expands,
filling space and time
until everything is pregnant.

And I know now
how we keep ourselves from this fullness—
how proud thoughts scatter us,
how riches bring us to famine,
how ruling over others keeps us from service,
how from generation to generation
we seek but cannot find
the promise that fired the hearts
of Abraham and Sarah.

I look around.
Mary is gone.
Her work is done.
She has been called
to guide
another singer of her song.

Without her presence and protection,
the clamor returns to claim me,
to sever my world, body,
 mind, and heart
from one another,
to reduce me to chaos,
to deny my identity,
to blur my mission.

Only the memory of her hand in mine
keeps me aware
that I am meant to cooperate with the love
that is reshaping the world.

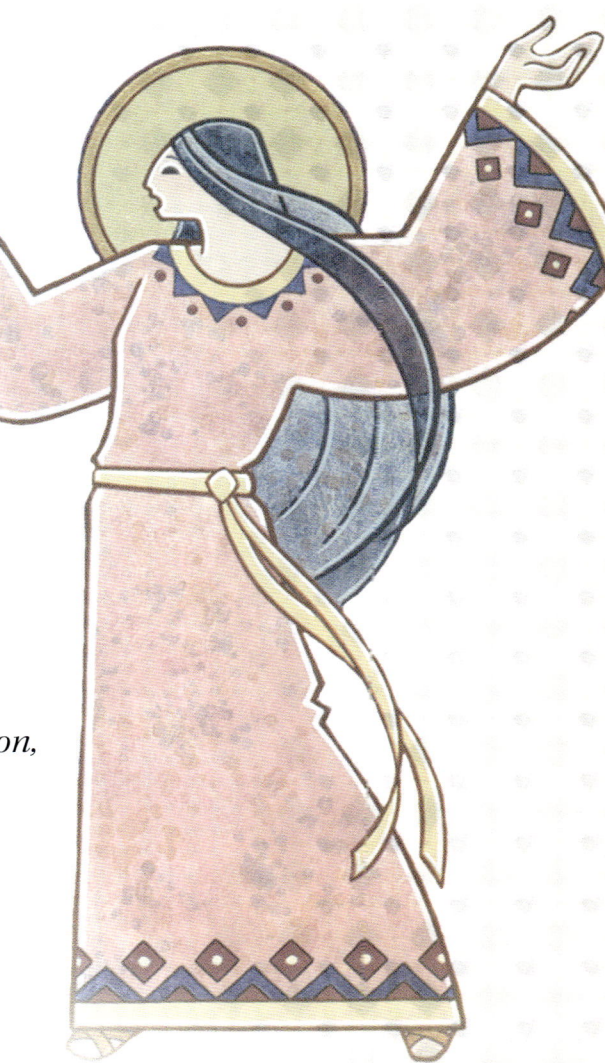

Luke 1:67–79

Then Zechariah his father, filled with the holy Spirit, prophesied, saying:

"Blessed be the Lord, the God of Israel,
    for he has visited and brought redemption to his people.
He has raised up a horn for our salvation
    within the house of David his servant,
even as he promised through the mouth of his holy prophets from of old:
    salvation from our enemies and from the hand of all who hate us,
to show mercy to our fathers
    and to be mindful of his holy covenant
and of the oath he swore to Abraham our father,
    and to grant us that, rescued from the hand of enemies,
without fear we might worship him in holiness and righteousness
    before him all our days.
And you, child, will be called prophet of the Most High,
    for you will go before the Lord to prepare his ways,
to give his people knowledge of salvation
    through the forgiveness of their sins,
because of the tender mercy of our God
    by which the daybreak from on high will visit us
to shine on those who sit in darkness and death's shadow,
    to guide our feet into the path of peace."

When I sing the song of Zachary
I remember
how silence was imposed upon him,
forcing an inner journey
that slowly wrung from him
exalted praise for promise-keeping.

The angel Gabriel appeared to Zachary
as he performed his priestly duties
in the Holy of Holies.
Bursting with good news,
the angel told him
his prayers had been answered:
his wife, Elizabeth, would bear a son.
The angel went on and on about the boy
until it became clear,
even to the frightened Zachary,
that his priestly loins
would produce a prophet.

But years of unanswered prayers
    make a man suspicious.
So Zachary told the angel
he was unconvinced.
Biological laws do not bend,
and he and Elizabeth were beyond child-bearing.
"How will I know that this is so?"

Angels do not take it well
when their messages are questioned.
Gabriel reminded Zachary
that angels belong to a higher order
whose ways the children of earth
can never completely comprehend.
So the best preparation
to celebrate the birth of his son
was muteness,
a discipline that would bring him
to deeper understanding.

*So the sentence of silence began,
and it is those nine months of speechlessness
that I ponder
as I prepare to sing the canticle
that finally flowed from his heart
when John was born.*

*At first, Zachary goes home into
    a frantic world of signs,
his eyes pleading for someone to interpret his hands
or to wait upon his slow scratches of writing.
But soon he calms,
and does no more than watch Elizabeth
become heavy with what he cannot understand.
In this space of silent contemplation,
beyond the mind's addiction to evidence,
he hears whispered words
coming from deep within him.
He descends after them
until the faint sounds sharpen.*

*Then, like a long withheld fulfillment,
like a promise being kept in a way never expected,
the dawn from on high breaks through his darkness.
The tender mercy of God cradles him,
the way of peace opens before him.*

*He eats the fruit of silence
and his soul begins to compose.
His mouth opens in a laugh
    that cannot be heard.
He and Elizabeth are
    symbiotically pregnant,
a child growing inside her,
a song growing inside him.
Both will be born together.*

There lived in Jerusalem at the time a certain man named Simeon. He was just and pious, and awaited the consolation of Israel, and the Holy Spirit was upon him. It was revealed to him by the Holy Spirit that he would not experience death until he had seen the Anointed of the Lord. He came to the temple now, inspired by the Spirit; and when the parents brought in the child Jesus to perform for him the customary ritual of the law, he took him in his arms and blessed God in these words:

"Now, Master, you can dismiss your servant in peace;
    you have fulfilled your word.
For my eyes have witnessed your saving deed
    displayed for all the peoples to see:
A revealing light to the Gentiles,
    the glory of your people Israel."

The child's father and mother were marveling at what was being said about him. Simeon blessed them and said to Mary his mother: "This child is destined to be the downfall and the rise of many in Israel, a sign that will be opposed—and you yourself shall be pierced with a sword—so that the thoughts of many hearts may be laid bare."

When I sing the canticle of Simeon,
I envy his privileged place in salvation history.
His aged eyes see the child of promise,
his ears hear the infant cry of the Savior.
This allows him to go in peace,
to take leave of life.
Fulfillment has arrived.

How many have wanted
to be able to say,
"Now you can dismiss
your servant in peace"?

I think of a friend who died
while his children were still young.
As I sat at his bedside,
he was agitated and unable to talk.
I asked him
if he was worried about his wife and children.
He nodded.
I told him they would miss him,
   but they would do well.
He held up his hand
with the index and middle fingers crossed,
the sign for "Hope so!"
No song of Simeon for him.

We know how deep bargaining goes in us—
the parent prays to stay alive
until a child is married or a grandchild is born.
We hope that when our time comes,
it will be the right time and we will be ready.
We will have partaken of a feast
that so satisfies our hunger and thirst that
no more will be needed.
Then our fist will open
and we will let go.
We will surrender without regret
and lay down the burden of our days.
May it be so!

*But I am not sure.
I was told of a spiritual teacher
who, after a heart attack,
invited one of his students to his house.
When the student arrived,
the teacher met him at the door
wearing his hat and coat.
They walked down the street
to a neighborhood bar.
Inside every table was full:
people were eating, drinking, and laughing.
The teacher turned to his student and said,
"See."*

*For many of us,
for me,
there may be no resolution within life,
no culmination of our efforts.
We may die unfulfilled, with work undone,
with others carrying on without us,
with a sense of loss so profound that
no hope,
in this world or the next,
can completely calm us.
We exit in mid-party,
untimely ripped.
It is just the way it is.
"See."*

*But if there is a chance
to make Simeon's words our last song,
we must radicalize ourselves as servants.
It is the servant who seeks dismissal
    after accomplishment;
all the rest of us merely stop—
abruptly or gradually.
If we have given our life
to God and other people,
we may know Spirit well enough
to trust its unfoldings.
If we can open to this trust,
we will sense support
and dare to suspect that
we and the people we love
are held by larger arms.
Our heritage of service will sustain us
as our bodies fail us.
We will depart in peace,
knowing that the One we have served
is faithful
in ways beyond our ability to imagine.*

John 1:1-18

In the beginning was the Word,
> and the Word was with God,
> and the Word was God.
He was in the beginning with God.
> All things came to be through him,
> and without him nothing came to be.
What came to be through him was life,
> and this life was the light of the human race;
the light shines in the darkness,
> and the darkness has not overcome it.

> A man named John was sent from God. He came for testimony, to testify to the light, so that all might believe through him. He was not the light, but came to testify to the light. The true light, which enlightens everyone, was coming into the world.

He was in the world,
> and the world came to be through him,
> but the world did not know him.
He came to what was his own,
> but his own people did not accept him.

> But to those who did accept him he gave power to become children of God, to those who believe in his name, who were born not by natural generation nor by human choice nor by a man's decision but of God.

And the Word became flesh
> and made his dwelling among us,
> and we saw his glory,
> the glory as of the Father's only Son,
> full of grace and truth.

> John testified to him and cried out, saying, "This was he of whom I said, 'The one who is coming after me ranks ahead of me because he existed before me.'" From his fullness we have all received, grace in place of grace, because while the law was given through Moses, grace and truth came through Jesus Christ. No one has ever seen God. The only Son, God, who is at the Father's side, has revealed him.

When I sing this canticle of the Eternal Word,
I lay the individual words
like seeds upon my heart.
As I ponder their meaning,
they sink and take root.
When they grow, they carry me with them.

There is always a Word coming forth,
always an unfolding,
always an inner fullness spilling over,
like a wedding with too much wine,
like a net with too many fish,
like a slow waterfall of perfume
    from an alabaster vase,
its fragrance filling the whole world.
As it flows, it creates.

Through this Word the cosmos is intricately built up,
nesting layer within layer,
spiraling, weaving, generating, pulsing.
All that was, is, and will be
hums with the life of this Word.

And then this Word
entered into one man,
dwelt and flowered in him,
a tree that could bear fruit in any season.

He was grace and truth,
the light of God for our darkness,
a light that the darkness, no matter its intrigue,
could not extinguish.
He showed us a place in ourselves
beyond the dictates of the blood,
beyond the desires of the flesh,
beyond the ambitions of a man,
a place where a child of God
is born out of the energies of love.

In him the One Word broke into many words,
as a man would take one loaf of bread
and, breaking it, offer it to all—
the gift of fullness from which all receive.

He became a word of compassion:
  "He approached the victim,
    poured oil and wine over his wounds
    and bandaged them" (Luke 10:34).

He became a word of encouragement:
  "You are not far from the Kingdom of God"
  (Mark 12:34).

He became a word of welcome:
  "While he was still a long way off,
    his father caught sight of him, and . . . ran"
    (Luke 15:20).

He became every word the human heart
  longs to hear.

Most of all, he became a word of love:
  "No one has greater love than this,
    to lay down one's life for one's friends.
    You are my friends" (John 15:13).

And he entered the dark night of our death,
  flesh of our flesh, brother of our fear,
  revealing God's love for us
  that he heard at the Father's side.

When I have finished this song
and the seed-words have grown,
I stretch out my arms like branches
and imagine myself a tree
in which all the birds of the air
can find a home.

Philippians 2:5-11

Have among yourselves the same attitude
that is also yours in Christ Jesus,

Who, though he was in the form of God,
    did not regard equality with God
        something to be grasped.
Rather, he emptied himself,
    taking the form of a slave,
    coming in human likeness;
    and found human in appearance,
    he humbled himself,
    becoming obedient to death,
        even death on a cross.
Because of this, God greatly exalted him
    and bestowed on him the name
    that is above every name,
    that at the name of Jesus
    every knee should bend,
    of those in heaven and on earth and under the earth,
    and every tongue confess that
    Jesus Christ is Lord,
    to the glory of God the Father.

When I sing this canticle of the mind of Christ Jesus
and take seriously the injunction
that we should put it on,
making his mind our own,
I know that I am overmatched,
and ready myself for a life of repentance
in the face of a challenge
that will never go away.

Our minds are not empty bowls
waiting to receive the wine of this revelation.
Our minds are tape libraries,
playing one scenario after another,
 thoughts thinking themselves,
      dragging us into romance, wealth,
        and world domination.
       Our fantasies leave no room
        for this Christ-mind that refuses to cling
         to any God who does not
         serve and die.

We are always looking for an edge,
exploiting whatever we can for our own advantage,
muscling for the first place at table,
angling for the salutation in the marketplace,
demanding an exemption
from what lesser folk have to endure.
Privilege is our food and drink.
Can we wake from these ego dramas?

Jesus showed us the way of the foot washer.
As water is poured into a basin,
we can pour ourselves out in service
and join with God's self-giving
that will make us spiritually more
even as we become socially less.
Knees only bend in homage at the name of Jesus
because his own knees first bent over scarred feet.

*But can we sing this song
as our own?*

*What other images of God
have taken up residence
in our minds?
What of the Sender of plagues, famines,
    and pestilence?
What of the Commander of armies of angels,
the Seeker of revenge, the Eternal Torturer?
If we go with Christ Jesus,
who will make our enemies
the footstools under our feet?
The foot washer has no interest
in this type of furniture arrangement.*

*Therefore, to sing this song,
we must leave much behind.
We must tire of domination,
be bone weary of vengeance,
too exhausted to rage.*

*Then our tongues will be free
to confess the name that is above every name,
the name of love,
and we will know
there is no other God
and there is no other way.*

*But when in the grip of fallen logic,
our minds forget this—
and they will—
then sing the canticle of the mind of Christ
and once again
be led into the light,
into the challenge
that will never go away.*

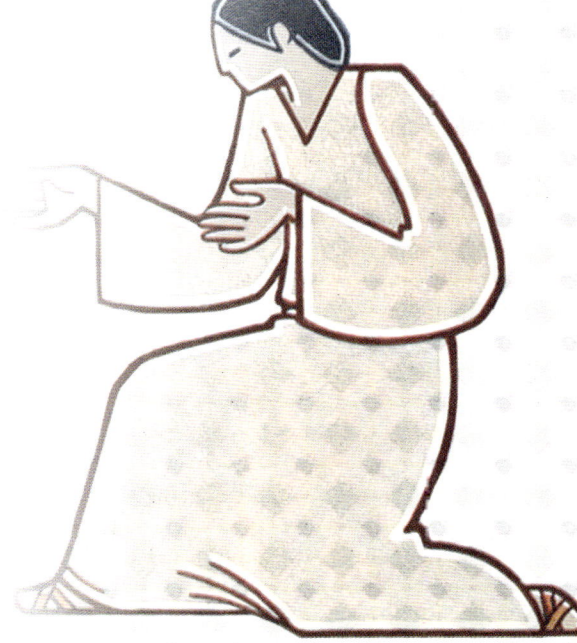

Colossians 1:12-20

[Give] thanks to the Father, who has made you fit to share in the inheritance of the holy ones in light. He delivered us from the power of darkness and transferred us to the kingdom of his beloved Son, in whom we have redemption, the forgiveness of sins.

He is the image of the invisible God,
    the firstborn of all creation.
For in him were created all things in heaven and on earth,
    the visible and the invisible,
        whether thrones or dominions or principalities or powers;
    all things were created through him and for him.
He is before all things,
    and in him all things hold together.
He is the head of the body, the church.
He is the beginning, the firstborn from the dead,
    that in all things he himself might be preeminent.
For in him all the fullness was pleased to dwell,
    and through him to reconcile all things for him,
    making peace by the blood of his cross
        [through him], whether those on earth or those in heaven.

When I sing this canticle,
my mind latches on to the "double" firstborn,
firstborn of all creation and firstborn from the dead.
He is the initial coming forth
of both creation and new creation.

Firstborn is a prestigious title.
But it means more than number one,
more than preeminent status,
more than Christ's hierarchical position
as imaging the Invisible Source
and reigning over creation and church.

The firstborn is a starter,
the one who makes possible
secondborns, thirdborns, and fourthborns.
He is the one who begins and sustains something new.
The essence of the firstborn
is to look down the line.

What made the early Christians
call Christ firstborn?

I remember
when the disciples were in a boat,
whipped by night winds,
and they saw him coming to them upon the waves.
They thought he was a ghost;
and even after Jesus assured them it was him,
they were not sure.
So Peter said, "Lord, if it is you,
command me come to you on the water"
    (Matthew 14:28).
Peter knew that if it was the firstborn
he would give all he had
to one who desired him to be a secondborn.
The firstborn said, "Come!"
Of course, Peter sank.
But the wave-walking Christ
rescued him,
giving him instructions
for another try.

*Jesus also said,
"I came so that they might have life,
and have it more abundantly" (John 10:10).
This is an outrageous firstborn sentiment,
making others the sole reason for his being.
The hymn tells us how this is possible.
"For in him all the fullness was pleased to dwell."
His self-giving was not out of scarce resources.
He never feared burnout.
Nor was his giving
an effort or obligation or sacrifice.
It was pleasure and flow,
a way of being for others
that dwelling in fullness makes possible.
This is the thing about firstborns:
even as they give birth to secondborns,
they never leave the source
from which they came.
Every emptying of themselves
opens them to a greater filling.*

◆━━━●◆●━━━━━◆

*Where does that leave us
who sing the praises of
    the firstborn?*

*We must learn to receive
what he so desperately wants
    to give.
This is more difficult
than our fantasies imagine.
Take Peter, again.
When the firstborn poured water in a basin
and approached his feet,
he adamantly refused.
"You will never wash my feet" (John 13:8).
Peter was more comfortable
with a Lord who wanted to be worshiped
than with a firstborn who wanted to share.*

*Becoming a secondborn
is a difficult birth.
We will have to sing this hymn
more than once.*

1 Timothy 3:16

Undeniably great is the mystery of devotion:

He was manifested in the flesh,
    vindicated in the spirit;
Seen by the angels,
    preached among the Gentiles,
Believed in throughout the world,
    taken up into glory.

When I sing this canticle of bullet points,
I feel that I have been handed an executive summary
and my first instinct is to ask,
"Could someone kindly gloss this?"

The phrases of this song beg for elaboration.
But that is how it should be.
The best expressions of faith
are those that take us
to the mountaintop of mystery
and leave us looking at the sky.
They point more than they explain.
Cryptic is their virtue.

The Mystery behind the words
and carried by the words
must never be dissolved.
Every revelation must include concealment.
We cannot delude ourselves into thinking
we have captured in concepts
what is beyond the finite net of our minds.
When our minds confess what they know,
they must also confess what they do not know.

The only thing the mystery of devotion makes clear
is that the horizon always recedes
as we approach it.
"Undeniably great is the mystery of devotion."

The greatness of this mystery of devotion
begins with the manifestation
of the beloved Son of the self-giving Father
in the full humanity of Jesus' flesh.
Everything Jesus says and does,
his dying and rising,
is how Spirit vindicates its love affair with flesh.
Divinity and humanity are love-locked partners
in the unfolding of salvation.

The mystery of devotion grows greater
as reception of this revelation grows broader.
Angels view this bringing together
of spirit and flesh,
this coming to pass
of the dream of creation.

Since they are pledged to carry out
  the divine intention,
they know complete accomplishment
when they see it.
They bow to the Son
who brought heaven to earth.

Not only the angels,
but all the Gentiles, the far-flung nations,
hear of this love affair
and come to believe in it.
The story is so attractive
it cannot be resisted.

And why should not the whole world believe in it?
The One who told it and lived it
now resides in the glory of God,
sharing the radiance that outshines the darkness,
a radiance that illumines the life of all.

And now we have sung
the mystery of our devotion.
With each phrase
its greatness has been revealed
and hidden.

The words we have used
are the gifts of our ancestors,
the provocative best they could do
as they devoted themselves
to the Mystery that was revealed among them.
We are their heirs,
doing the best we can with the same Mystery
as it continues to grow greater in its revelation.
Our failure to bring it
completely to words
is a sure sign of our fidelity.

Revelation 5:6-14

Then, between the throne with the four living creatures and the elders, I saw a Lamb standing, a Lamb that had been slain. He had seven horns and seven eyes; these eyes are the seven spirits of God, sent to all parts of the world. The Lamb came and received the scroll from the right hand of the One who sat on the throne. When he had taken the scroll, the four living creatures and the twenty-four elders fell down before the Lamb. Along with their harps, the elders were holding vessels of gold filled with aromatic spices, which were the prayers of God's holy people. This is the new hymn they sang:

"Worthy are you to receive the scroll
    and break open its seals,
    for you were slain.
With your blood you purchased for God
    those of every race and tongue,
    of every people and nation.
You made them a kingdom,
    and priests to serve our God,
    and they shall reign on the earth."

I looked again and heard the voices of many angels who surrounded the throne and the living creatures and the elders. They were countless in number, thousands and tens of thousands, and they all cried out:
"Worthy is the Lamb that was slain
    to receive power and riches, wisdom and strength,
    honor and glory and praise!"

Then I heard the voices of every creature in heaven and on earth and under the earth and in the sea; everything in the universe cried aloud:

"To the One seated on the throne, and to the Lamb,
    be praise and honor, glory and might,
    forever and ever!"

The four living creatures answered, "Amen," and the elders fell down and worshiped.

*When I enter into this ecstatic vision
and join every level of creation
in their thunderous hymn
to the worthiness of the Lamb,
I realize how much inner work I have to do
to let this canticle touch my spirit.*

*In the temple
people purchased lambs
and priests slaughtered them
to atone for sins.
Through this animal sacrifice
people who were alienated from God
were restored to righteousness.
The medium of their regained communion
was the blood of the lamb.*

*But Jesus,
as he did with everything he touched,
transformed this liturgy.
When he cleansed the temple,
he freed the animals—
no more lambs to slaughter.
Instead, he took their place.
He was the path of reconciliation with God.
He became the Lamb of God
who took away the sin of the world,
who reunited creation to its Source.*

*Therefore, is there a creature anywhere
who will not raise its voice in homage?*

*"Worthy is the Lamb that was slain
   to receive power and riches, wisdom and strength,
   honor and glory and praise!"*

*But these words of overwhelming praise
must come from a full heart.
If I sang them only because
the chorus of the earth had dragged me along,
the Lamb would remain worthy
but my singing would be unworthy.*

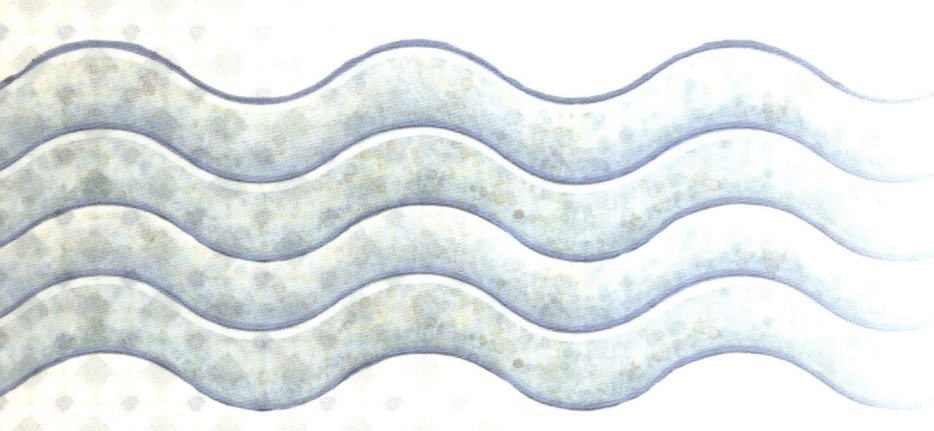

*So I go back to my youth,
when I first heard about him,
when the seed was first planted,
when parents, nuns, and priests,
in a delicate surgery of love,
placed heaven in my heart.*

*And I realize I cannot remember a time
when I did not know his revelation,
when his truth did not create tears
and the tears did not create flowers.*

*Even when I tried to shake him,
to lock him in a monstrance
where he would grow stale,
it was too late.
I could not conceive of any world
where love did not run toward us
in welcome.*

*It is only because
    I have been with him so long
that I know the secret of the scroll
that only the Lamb can open.
Like all great secrets,
it was never hidden,
only unable to be seen by the hardness of our hearts.
And then came the arsonist of the heart.*

*I do not know who I would have been
or what I would have become
had I not met
the Lamb slain from the foundation of the world.
I place that simple confession
in the golden bowl of incense.
Its rising smoke will carry my song,
a discordant yet faithful voice in the chorus of the earth.*

Alleluia! The Lord has established his reign, God, the Almighty. Let us rejoice and be glad and give him glory.

Revelation 19:6-7

Revelation 19:6-8

Then I heard something like the sound of a great multitude or the sound of rushing water or mighty peals of thunder, as they said:

> "Alleluia!
> The Lord has established his reign,
>   [our] God, the almighty.
> Let us rejoice and be glad
>   and give him glory.
> For the wedding day of the Lamb has come,
>   his bride has made herself ready.
> She was allowed to wear
>   a bright, clean linen garment."

When I sing this wedding canticle,
I do not sweat salvation
and wonder if I will be one of the band of brides
who will gleam in linen.
My deeds of righteousness
will not get me to the altar.
It is not about being worthy
to be chosen as a bride.

Instead, I ask
what is this strange wedding
that takes place when
"the Lamb has come,
his bride has made herself ready."

There is a Nordic tale
in which a young and feisty princess
is attracted to a golden wreath
that a great white bear twirls around its paw.
The golden wreath is the fullness of
human potential
and the great white bear symbolizes
the goodness and strength that can bestow it.
She asks the bear
what she will have to give
to get the wreath.
She does not wait for an answer,
but quickly offers
jewels, crowns, and suchlike
that princesses have lying around
as a swap for the wreath.
But the bear responds:
"To get this golden wreath
you will have to give yourself.
You will have to marry me."

*That is what marriage to the Lamb is:
not an exchange of something we have,
a* quid pro quo *arrangement,
but an intercourse of selves,
the coming together of a greater strength
    and goodness
with a human openness that is
    looking for fulfillment.*

*The greater strength and goodness of the Lamb
is the self-giving of God revealed in Christ.
The Lamb is a groom of true love,
whose only desire is to complete his bride,
to allow his Spirit to so enflame her beauty
that deeds of righteousness radiate from her.
This divine initiative of the Lamb,
the outpouring of grace,
turns every soul, male and female, feminine.
At a level beneath ordinary awareness
we know our bridal role
is to welcome God's embrace.*

*The wedding day is every Sunday.
No matter what we wear
we are clothed in "a bright, clean linen garment."
We eliminate the traffic of everyday affairs
and put our mind in our heart,
where the fire of love melts resistance.
Then we come forward in readiness,
our mouths open
or our hands out.
We receive,
without reserve or reticence,
the Body of Christ,
the groom.
The marriage of the Lamb
    is consummated.*

About the art

The twenty paintings that I created for *Canticle* are visual meditations on biblical texts. The paintings were inspired both by the imagery evoked by the scriptures themselves and by the narrative approach of the frescoes and paintings of medieval European masters such as Giotto and Fra Angelico, with which I have long been fascinated.

I chose to incorporate a passage from the scriptural text in the border of each painting to serve as a unifying element among the twenty works. The two-dimensional perspective and rich color also echo the style and technique of medieval painting. The artworks were executed in acrylic paints on archival rag board.

—G. E. Mullan

G. E. Mullan draws on his academic background in both art and theology to express two thousand years of Christian tradition in a unique contemporary style. His religious art reveals a synthesis of such diverse artistic traditions as the imagery of the Roman catacombs, the icons and mosaics of the Italo-Byzantine world, the illuminated manuscripts of medieval Europe, and the Santos of Mexico and the American Southwest. In compositions noted for their use of lyrical line set against an ordered and complex geometry of interdependent shapes, he presents his view of timeless Christian faith.

Religious institutions have commissioned him to create numerous works, one of which was an official gift from the Archdiocese of San Antonio to Pope John Paul II on the occasion of the 1987 papal visit to Texas. He was one of the artists who represented the archdiocese at the Jubilee for Artists as part of the Vatican 2000 Jubilee celebration.

He resides with his wife, Celina, in San Antonio, Texas.

John Shea is a theologian and storyteller who lectures nationally and internationally on storytelling in world religions, faith-based health care, contemporary spirituality, and the spirit at work movement. Among other things, he has been professor of systematic theology and Director of the Doctor of Ministry Program at the University of St. Mary of the Lake, and a research professor at the Institute of Pastoral Studies at Loyola University of Chicago. He has published numerous books of theology and spirituality and several books of poetry. Among his books are *Gospel Light: Jesus Stories for Spiritual Consciousness* (Crossroad, 1997), *Elijah at the Wedding Feast and Other Tales* (Acta Press, 1999), *Stopping Along the Way: Stations of the Cross* (World Library Publications, 2005), and *The Spiritual Wisdom of the Gospels for Christian Preachers and Teachers: Year A, Year B, Year C,* (Liturgical Press, 2004, 2005, 2006).

He and his wife live in River Forest, Illinois.